Nothing but Love and Lace

An Interactive Experience of Passion Poetry

Kc Gloer

GALLIVANT PRESS

Copyright © 2024 by Kc Gloer

Interior design by Julie Pershing

All rights reserved.

No part of this book may be reproduced in any form or by any electronic or mechanical means, including information storage and retrieval systems, without written permission from the author, except for the use of brief quotations in a book review.

Paperback ISBN: 978-1-947894-39-6

Printed in USA

To True Love

For the love shared between two hearts, the kind that grows stronger with every whispered word and every tender touch.

This book is for the moments when you look into each other's eyes and feel everything you can't quite say.

May these poems bring you closer, reminding you of the magic that happens when two souls connect deeply, passionately, and with *Nothing but Love and Lace*.

With Love Always,

Kc Gloer

Table of Contents

Foreword -- **vii**

Anticipation --**9**

Anticipation	11
Let's Go!	13
A Rose for You	15
New Beginnings	17
Feeling at Home	19
Looking for Fun	21
I am Ready	23
You Kiss	25
Before Now Fades Away	27
Forbidden	29
Reflections	31

Tenderness-- **33**

Carefree Love	35
Playing for You	37
Harmony	39
Rainbows and Rain	41
Cherish	43
The Finest Wine	45
Waiting	47
Reflections Illuminating	49
Completely	51
Midnight Passion	53
Reflections	55

Passion — 57

Tenderness to Passion	59
Again and Again	61
Lovely to be a Woman	63
I Need You, Now!	65
Threads of Gold	67
Make Love to Me	69
Taste of Ecstasy	71
With Passion	73
Rhythm of Love	75
Moments of Passion	77
Reflections	81

Love — 83

Light is the Air	85
I Feel Loved	87
Sit with Me	89
Just Be	91
Once in a Lifetime Dance	93
We Are One	95
The One I love	97
Your Beautiful Life	99
Sweet Serenity	101
True Love	103
Reflections	105

Acknowledgments — 109
About the Author — 111
Also by Kc Gloer — 113
Connect with Kc Gloer — 115

Foreword

Nothing but Love and Lace is more than just a collection of poems; it's a journey meant to be taken together, a way to reconnect with the love that brought you and your partner together in the first place.

When I first envisioned this book, I imagined couples curled up together, reading these poems to each other. I wanted each verse to feel like a love letter, letting the emotions they inspire draw you even closer. These poems are designed to be shared—to open new avenues of communication, to remind you of the warmth and passion you share, and to bring a renewed sense of intimacy to your relationship.

This book is all about slowing down and being present with each other. In our busy lives, it's easy to forget to say those sweet things or to take the time to appreciate the love you share. These poems are here to help you do just that—to reconnect, reignite, and remind you why you fell in love in the first place.

So as you read these poems, take your time. Let each one be a reminder of the love you cherish and the bond that continues to grow between you. May this book become a part of your shared story, something you return to whenever you want to feel that closeness and connection.

Discover the beauty in each chapter of your love story,
one verse at a time.

Anticipation

Anticipation

Feeling your breath
That moment before we kiss
Anticipation explodes
Your body knows
I am yours

Let's Go!

Embracing comfort
Resting and waiting
Eagerly anticipating
Getting ready to shine
No more time to waste
It is time to let go
Be free of the old
Be daring, be bold
It's time
Let's Go!

A Rose for You

A rose
Delicately sweet
Here for you
Until we meet
An atmosphere of love
Breathes with you everywhere

New Beginnings

It is time to let go
Embrace the good in your life
Keep moving forward
Anticipating
Excitement and joy
Adventure and love
Do not regret

Everything
Brought you to this point
Forgiveness heals your soul
Through love we rise
Bitterness we die
Lend a hand when you can

Be open to receiving
Don't try to go it alone
You will be amazed
By the love
Just waiting for you
Don't hesitate, don't wait
Seize every moment

Feeling at Home

Sit with me
Savor this moment
Waterfall cascading from the pond
Breathing in life
Sweet succulent scents
Deep conversation
Where secrets are kept
Where friendships are sealed

Looking for Fun

Wandering in the dark
Wondering if I would see
A pathway through the fog
A light shining just for me

I ventured forward
Slowly but unafraid
Music in the distance
Haze began to fade

Now walking faster
Anticipation of what I'll find
Humming and some laughter
Joyfully, I begin to unwind

People dancing everywhere
Friendly faces I see
This is what I was hoping for
Time to let go and be free!

I Am Ready

Sometimes sweet
Sometimes mellow
It flows between my lips
Around my tongue
I have waited for this moment
To hold and smell your rich fragrance
To see this shimmering color
Deepest red
Through its magnificence
Oh, the warmth of this potion
Seduction of its power
Now I am ready
Ready to fall under your spell
Take me to that place
Where an evening to remember awaits

You Kiss

Gently you hold her face
Your palms warm and caring
Ever so lightly your lips brush hers
Nothing more, just that gentle touch

You kiss
Over and over
Moistening her cheek
Her neck
Breathing, exhaling

You kiss
Lips continue to meet
No exploration just lips on lips
Softly, tenderly, slowly
Building, wanting, knowing

You kiss
Always let her breathe
Your tenderness is enough
To take her breath away
As you begin to hold her closer

You feel the anticipation
As you kiss

Before Now Fades Away

How delicately fresh
Simply elegant and true
Savor this scent
You know what to do

Caress with care
This moment won't last
Don't think, just act
You better move very fast

Don't live in the past
Wait for that moment
React with abandon
Act now with intent!

We have now
Please live for today
Yes, we have NOW!
Before now fades away...

Forbidden

Forbidden stirs desire
Wanting all the more
Feeding passions fire
Crossing through that door

Wondering what's in store
Anticipation nears its peak
Keeping secrets for
One you dare to seek

Words softly speak
Hungrily closing in
Lips brushing my cheek
Seizing what's forbidden

Reflections

Reflections

Tenderness

With Love

Carefree Love

I loved you then
Remembering to this day
Our laughter so deep
How we always had fun
We laid under the stars
Only holding hands
We played in the lake
With you holding my waist
We dug our feet in the sand
You kissed me, then again
Tender and gentle
More skilled then your years
I felt so warm
With the heat of the sun
Your lips so sweet
Your eyes so blue
Oh, how I remember
Being in love with you

Playing for You

On a bed of grass I play for you
With the breeze gently blowing
Words start flowing
I play for you

With the sun setting, I sing for you
Emotions from my fingertips
Caressing you with soft sweet lips
I sing for you

The wind is strong, I dance for you
Feeling excitement, I move along
Freedom of passion, free of wrong
I dance for you

With the warmth of night, I long for you
To touch my skin, to stroke my hair
Unraveling my secrets, my soul to bare
I long for you

As I play my song for you

Harmony

Roses grow
In the harmony of love
Where water flows deep
Where tenderness keeps
Its fragrance floating above

Rainbows and Rain

Give me a second to ease your pain
Tell me your story, why you feel this way
Rest your head on my chest tonight
My heart beating strong, rhythm brings calm

I'll touch you with kindness, with the softest
of hands
I'll whisper with gentleness, my voice will soothe
I'll kiss you with tenderness, with lips that care
I'll fill you with forgiveness, with a heart of tears

No more to look back on what cannot
be changed
No more to cry of days gone by
You cannot undo what's already been done
You can only lose, if you can't see the sun

Open your eyes to the beginning of a new day
Think of tomorrow, exciting in so many ways
Rainbows and rain, sunshine and love
Forgive what's been done and live life with love

Cherish

Waiting for you
Vulnerable
Wanting to feel
Wanting to be loved
To be touched
Cherished
Gently, tenderly
Giving back the love
I long to receive

The Finest Wine

Let your fingers be hungry
While your mouth explores gently
Your lips slightly parted
Gliding your tongue against mine
Savoring the flavors
Like a fine sip of wine
Slowly and carefully
Taking your time
Your hands intertwined
In the strands of my hair
My hands on your face
Gently caressing with care
Your hips against my hips
As you pull me even closer
Still, so tenderly kissing
Treating me as fragile as glass
Seducing my mind
My body, my all
Surrendering completely
When you love so sweetly
Taking you deeply
Heaven releasing
Showing you too
The joy of this feeling

Waiting

Life surrounds my being
Blessed by angels
Disguised as doves
Anticipating
Waiting
This night of love

Reflections Illuminating

I feel you touch me
In the breeze of the wind
I feel you near me
Whispering
How it's going to begin

Your breath is sweet
Your hand reaches out
Together we meet
Tenderness
Is what this is about

Strengthening our bond
Closeness is near
Succulent is the rose
Resting now in my palm
Serenity consuming, dissipating fear

This night now blooming
Upon dreams in twilight
Coming to life
Illuminating
Reflections in the moonlight

Completely

Kissing passionately
Quiet
Darkness is upon us
Your lips are gentle
Yet
Your strength, your body
Surrounds me
Then
Your tenderness overpowers me
I surrender completely, sweetly

Midnight Passion

The breeze is blowing
Gently through my window
Lights turned very low
Music softly playing
Lavender mist
Floats in the air
Silky silver sheets
Cool to the touch
Sipping Merlot
While swaying to and fro
Your chest against mine
Your hands on my hips
While your breath is teasing
Your lips are seducing
Passionately...we kiss

Reflections

Reflections

Tenderness to Passion

To lay with you
To touch you
Rhythms of the night
Chill of anticipation
Silk caressing my body
Heaving up and down
With each intense breath
Incredible tenderness
Your hand barely touches me
Gliding across my skin
Sweetness of your kisses
Upon my wanting shoulder
Warmth rising from within
Getting ready for the storm
Music so alive
Exciting me, seducing me
Your tongue is wet and wild
Tenderness to passion
Just like I imagined
Crossing the boundary
Without even knowing
How it all began

Again and Again

Deep deep blues
Soon fade away
My mind relaxes
Thinking of you
Resting on your chest
My body is longing
For your passionate touch
Holding me close
Our legs intertwined
Closer still
Until emotions unwind
Then all is still
Beating hearts
We hear
Nighttime settling in
Time to say goodbye
Until we meet again

Lovely to be a Woman

The beauty of a woman
Shines from inside
When she is free to be
Glowing and strong
Her energy will transform you
Her passion will consume you
Oh, how she will love
Oh, how she will adore you
When she is free, free to be
All she was meant to be!

I Need You, Now!

Touch me madly
Reach my soul
Mend my pieces
Make me whole

Ravish my mind
My body, my all
I need you now
Do you feel me call?

Anticipating, waiting
Passion intense
I feel you near
Your energy I sense

Entering
Now we're here
No words do we say
Gripping tight

Into my lair
Tangled not trapped
Dropping my towel
No longer wrapped

Naked we stand
Immersed as one
Time to be free
Desires have won

Weaving our web
Fiercely, delicate, and strong
Creating our rhythm
Slowly, deliberately along

Unaware yet acutely present
The day now past
Only now is relevant
Gliding, riding slow to fast

Expressing not hiding
Sounds of joy
Freedom alive
Amplified

Smiling, dripping
Not shy or coy
Nature's secrets
Ours to hold

Threads of Gold

Golden lace rests
Upon my breast
Caressing my flesh
Waiting for you
Saving my best
When you come to me
You will know
Intimacy you crave
Finally letting go
Exploring what's under
Those threads of gold
Lace upon lace
I look at your face
Ecstasy is near
Pleasure I hear
Coming together
Sounds of delight
Transcending
Passions of the night

Make Love to Me

Make love to me upon the sunrise
Make love to me when you're vibrantly alive
Make love in all your vibrancy
Make love to me in the vibrant sea
Make love to me as I vibrantly see
Your glowing soul vibrantly free
Make love to me deliciously sweet
Make love to me where our vibrancy meets
Bouncing through clouds
Rolling on the earth
Tasting the rainbows
Clawing in the dirt
Whispering, shouting alive so alive
Vibrantly you are becoming
The ocean you dreamed
Make love to me in a sea of pearls
Pearls you created
While making love to me
Seeing your vibrant reflection
Mirrors holding memories
Seeing while gazing
Eyes upon my eyes
I see you
Crystal clear
Vibrancy Vitality Victoriously Alive
I see you

Taste of Ecstasy

Come
Be naked with me
When the moon is high
When reflections shine
In your magnificent eyes
Watching your silhouette
Move closer
Seducing
Hypnotizing
Naked
In the moonlight
I reach for you
You reach back
Touching my spine
Kissing my neck
Passion increases
Desires releasing
Opening
The secret door
Revealing what only
You've been waiting for
This night is yours

Powerfully you hold me
Adore me
In the moonlight
I taste you on my lips
I taste your fingertips
I taste all of you
As you gaze at the moon
Then look back at me
Catching that moment
Intensely mine
Now you're there
On the edge and beyond
A rhythm only felt
While you're dancing within
Expressing your freedom
Together, we win
Flowing like wine
Ecstasies sweetness
Sleeping now
Into intimacies completeness

With Passion

We must not wait
Wait on tomorrow
No regrets
No feeling sorrow
With passion and purpose
Seize today
With the force of the wind
That carries you away
Not tomorrow
But today...

Rhythm of Love

You take me away
Away from pain and sadness
Bringing peace as I breathe
Breathing
Peace within
Listening to love's rhythm
Eyes now closed
I could be anywhere
Anywhere I choose
I choose the sounds of love
Inside this peace I have found
From you

Dedicated to Ian Maksin

Moments of Passion

Warmth abounds
Your gentle hands
Stroking my back
You have gone
Yet your touch remains

Taking me to a place
Only you could go
Transcending to a space
Only you and I would know
Boundless energy flows

Music playing in time
Seduced by the glint in your eye
Rhythm magnificently in tune
Undressing me where we lie
Hungrily tasting my wine

Passion is growing
Passion exploding
On the edge of ecstasy
On the edge of reality
Crescendo in full play

Ecstasies illusion
Vivid and real
Succumbing to forces
Beyond how you feel
Ecstasies illusion, here to stay

You play me beautifully
Waking up my senses
You play me skillfully
From your heart and soul
Studying carefully all delicate folds

Rising up, I greet you
Swaying perfectly, I see you
Deep and deeper, and deeper still
Your essence grows
This power I know

Sweetness of passion
Your lips so hot
Breathing your taste
With no time to waste
Again we rock and we rock

Devouring in wetness
Touching all senses
Reaching a depth
Never before explored
Giving me more of you to adore

Leaning back
You touch me and more
In the peak of desire
You set me on fire
Higher and higher, I soar

Falling together
Peacefully we rest
Savoring this moment
My head on your chest
A moment of passion
Always to remember

Reflections

Reflections

Love

Light is the Air

I give back to you
As you give to me
Feelings so sweet
Among the grass and trees
Roaming through
Fields of lavender
A breeze, warm
Light is the air
You blow through me

I Feel Loved

In dreams I danced
Days I dreamed
Romance and love
Ascending in sleep

Now my days
Fulfilled with dreams
Coming to life
In sparkling streams

Coming to life
With experiences savored
Open to feeling
Tasting its flavors

Romances now lived
Kisses so sweet
No longer living
Existing in dreams

Wonders abound
Life brand new
Blessed to be loved
By someone like you

Sit with Me

Come sit with me
Hold my hand
Inhale my love
Surrounding you
Breathe out your fear
Inside of you
You're not alone
I am sitting here too

Just Be

Come lay with me awhile
Hold me close, then closer
Breathe with me
Until we breathe as one

Let silence take over
No words to be spoken
Just being
All that matters is now

Now be present
To all that is
In this moment
In this embrace

Be still
Feeling every touch
Tender and passionate
Feeling hearts beat
Fiercely and sweet

Receiving, knowing
How special this is
Intimacy defined
Intimacy with our minds

Joining our bodies
Emotion exploding
Intimacy flowing
Into completeness we sigh

Once in a Lifetime Dance

Music of love playing
Seducing my mind
Seducing my all
I asked you to dance

It was a dance like no other
Taking me in your arms
Your cheek against mine
Not just close, closer

Feeling your heartbeat
Through your palms
As I held your hand
In harmony, in rhythm

Getting warmer as I feel your body
Guiding, swaying
Gripping tighter and tighter
I could not get close enough

Your breath, tickling my neck
Soon feeling your lips
I was intoxicated by you
Then, you kissed me

My eyes closed
Moving, receiving
The most passionate kiss of my life
Melting into you

Music in the distance
Time was no more
The world didn't exist
Except for this moment in time

Embraced, entranced
Enchanted
Mysteriously, totally
Completely

More than a kiss
More than an embrace
More than a dance
Forever, remembered
Without a trace

We are One

Together the night comes
We lie as one
Dreams visit for a time
Awakened with the sunlight
Together again, we rise!

The One I Love

You are the calm in my storm
My light when it's dark
My sun on a cloudy day
My rose blooming in the park

You are the warmth in the sand
My breath in my lungs
My blue of the sea
My tunes I have sung

You are the sweetness I drink
My strength when I'm weak
My river when I cry
My everything I seek

You are the one I love

Your Beautiful Life

If you pause
Just for a moment
Breathe in beauty
Breathe in calm

Let go of the pressure
Overwhelming your day
Too much to do?
Not enough time in the day

What's really important
Maybe a thing or two
Releasing the rest
Doesn't matter if you do

Spend time in love
Have fun, be free
Live in this moment
Let's all agree

A simpler life
Loving each other
Kindness will show
The way for others to go

Make today a day
One to remember
Tomorrow will come
Then it will be today

Another day
Another day
To love, to live
Your beautiful life today

Sweet Serenity

Divine divinity capturing creativity
Within our minds, within our souls
Oh peace becomes sweet serenity
Delivering grace so deeply traced
Ecstasy consuming this sacred place

True Love

Til the end of love, our love will be

Passions longing
Wanting
Belonging

Sweet as rain
Pure ecstasy

Never apart
Always being free

The only way, true love to be

Til the end of love, our love will be

Reflections

Reflections

Believe in Love

*If you believe in nothing else
Believe in Love*

*With Love,
Kc Gloer*

Acknowledgments

I want to extend my heartfelt gratitude to Lee Huffman who 'saw' me when I forgot who I was. Who lifted me and loved me when I didn't remember what that felt like. He was instrumental in helping me feel empowered and strong. Lee was my inspiration for some of the poems in *Nothing But Love and Lace*.

My deep appreciation to Kellie Grill for her love and forever friendship, her life altering workshops including working with her magnificent healing horses at her Ranch at Happiness Success Ranch Retreats where I experienced major breakthroughs in knowing my purpose in this world.

Kellie Grill, Master Equine Gestaltist
Happy Success Ranch Retreats

To Julia Helen, my best friend, and the keeper of my secrets—whether it's late at night or early in the morning, she's always there when I need her (we all need a friend like this). She is a constant source of support; going above and beyond for friends and family. True friendship isn't bound by time or distance—but by the heart.

About the Author

International Poet, Author, Speaker, Coach

Kc Gloer is an internationally recognized poet, author, speaker, and coach. She has dedicated her life to spreading hope, humanity, and love to others. Kc has touched the hearts of individuals around the world.

Kc's message of never giving up and her journey of resilience, courage, and grace has inspired many to find their own strength in difficult times.

Her words and actions embody hope and love, shining a light on a world that can often feel dark and overwhelming.

Through her writing, speaking, and coaching, Kc continues to make a positive impact on the lives of others, inspiring them to embrace their own resilience and to never give up. Join Kc on her journey of spreading hope, humanity, and love to create a brighter, more inspired world.

Also by Kc Gloer

Books:

Nothing But Lace
Nothing But Love and Lace

Kc's poems are included in the following International Poetry Collections and Anthologies:

International Poetry Collections:

Little Sparks of Joy - Curated by Chrisoula Sirigou
Mastering the Game of Life 2 - Curated by Paul D. Lowe

Anthologies:

Love Poems - Curated by Veronica Esagui
Magic Poems - Curated by Veronica Esagui
Mortality Poems - Curated by Veronica Esagui

Connect with Kc Gloer

Website:
https://ovegloriously.com/

Women's Retreats:
https://lovegloriously.com/retreats/

Email:
hello@lovegloriously.com

How You Can Help:
Leave a Review!

As an independent poet, I rely on the support of readers like you to share my work with others. If my words spoke to you, I'd be incredibly grateful if you left a positive review on Amazon.

Even a few words can help others discover this collection and appreciate the art of poetry.

Thank you for being a part of my journey.

Your Journey Begins Here...

Turn Your Passion into a Published Book

Bring your book to life—connect with us today!

hello@gallivantpress.com
www.gallivantpress.com

www.ingramcontent.com/pod-product-compliance
Lightning Source LLC
Chambersburg PA
CBHW070150080526
44586CB00015B/1926